iScience

Variables and Experiments:
Getting Across the River

by Emily Sohn and Frederick Fellows

Chief Content Consultant
Edward Rock
Associate Executive Director, National Science Teachers Association

NORWOOD HOUSE PRESS
Chicago, Illinois

Norwood House Press
PO Box 316598
Chicago, IL 60631

For information regarding Norwood House Press, please visit our website at
www.norwoodhousepress.com or call 866-565-2900.

Special thanks to: Amanda Jones, Amy Karasick, Alanna Mertens, Terrence Young, Jr.

Editors: Jessica McCulloch, Michelle Parsons, Diane Hinckley
Designer: Daniel M. Greene
Production Management: Victory Productions, Inc.

Library of Congress Cataloging-in-Publication data

Sohn, Emily.

Variables and experiments : getting across the river / by Emily Sohn and Frederick Fellows;
chief content consultant, Edward Rock.

p. cm.—(iScience readers)

Summary: "Describes how using variables and performing experiments, like
scientists do, can help find answers to questions. As readers use scientific
inquiry to problem solve on their own, an activity based on real world
situations challenges them to apply what they've learned in order to solve
a puzzle"—Provided by publisher.

Includes bibliographical references and index.

ISBN-13: 978-1-59953-431-2 (library edition: alk. paper)
ISBN-10: 1-59953-431-2 (library edition: alk. paper)

1. Science—Experiments—Juvenile literature. 2. Problem solving—Juvenile literature.
I. Fellows, Frederick. II. Rock, Edward. III. Title.

Q164.S595 2012
507.8—dc22
2011011702

CONTENTS

Note to Caregivers:

Throughout this book, many questions are posed to the reader. Some are open-ended and ask what the reader thinks. Discuss these questions with your child and guide him or her in thinking through the possible answers and outcomes. There are also questions posed which have a specific answer. Encourage your child to read through the text to determine the correct answer. Most importantly, encourage answers grounded in reality while also allowing imaginations to soar. Information to help support you as you share the book with your child is provided in the back in the **Additional Notes** section.

Words that are **bolded** are defined in the glossary in the back of the book.

Seeking Answers

What are some questions you think about? You might wonder how many books can fit in your backpack. Or maybe you want to know whether it will be hot enough tomorrow to wear shorts.

Scientists have a good way to answer questions. They perform **experiments.** They test ideas.

This book will help you figure out how to answer questions. You will learn to do your own experiments.

Water Crossing

Here's your chance to solve a problem like a scientist. Imagine you are standing on a riverbank. The river is wide but it isn't flowing fast. You want to build a tree house on the other side of the river. How can you best get yourself and your supplies across?

For this puzzle, you won't cross a real river. Instead, you will try to get a grapefruit across a container of water. Imagine that you are the grapefruit. A sink or a basin filled with water will be the river you are trying to cross.

Your job is to move the grapefruit from one side of the sink to the other without getting it wet. As you work your way through this book, you will get closer to the perfect solution.

Here is what you have to work with:
- deep sink (or basin) filled with 8 inches (20 centimeters) of water
- stack of newspapers
- glue
- ball of string
- empty half-liter plastic bottle
- scissors
- grapefruit (or other object of similar size and weight)

A large grapefruit weighs about 1 pound (½ kilogram). You cannot use your hands to touch the grapefruit to move it. Instead, you need to use the materials listed in the activity.

The perfect spot for a tree house is across the river. Think about how you can get yourself and your tree house supplies over to the other side easily, safely, and still dry.

Think about some of the puzzle's challenges. In the real world, construction materials for a tree house cost a lot. So you want to use as few supplies as possible. You should also move quickly. You are eager to get started on your tree house. And you want to be safe. You don't want your grapefruit (you!) to fall into the water! What else do you need to think about?

There are several possible strategies for crossing a river. Swimming is one way. Taking a boat is another. Crossing a bridge is a third. All strategies have upsides and downsides. Swimming would get you there faster than if you first made a boat from scratch. But you'll eventually need materials to build the tree house, and a boat could carry them. You also probably wouldn't get as cold on a boat as you might if you swam.

Why might it be helpful to build a bridge to cross the river? What are the downsides of building a bridge? Consider cost, time, and safety.

Floating across in a boat would be a good idea, if you had a boat. But you don't. At least, not yet.

People have come up with lots of ways to cross rivers. Some strategies require careful planning and a lot of hard work. Sometimes, the work is dangerous.

When scientists begin to solve problems, they brainstorm, or list as many ideas as they can. Write down or draw all of your ideas for crossing the river. They can be as wild as swinging like a monkey or as practical as laying a plank across the river.

How many ideas did you have? Which would be the quickest? Which would be the safest? Which would cost the least?

How might you test your ideas to see which one is best?

Paper-Thin Strength

You might want to build something to cross the river. Try this activity to see how a structure can be stronger than its parts.

Materials
- piece of paper
- scissors
- tape
- large slim book

How strong are paper tubes? You're going to find out!

Fold a piece of paper in half so it is long and skinny. Fold it in half again. Open up the paper and cut along the three folds. Now you have four even strips of paper.

Roll each strip into a short, loosely formed tube. Use a few pieces of tape to keep each tube closed. Do you think these paper tubes can hold weight?

Balance all four tubes so they are standing and together form a rectangle. What do you think will happen if you place a book on top?

You can use building materials to make all kinds of things. The key is to tap into their strengths.

Write down your **prediction.** As you perform the experiment, write what happens next to your predictions. Now, gently place the book on the paper tubes. If you arrange them right, the tubes should hold up the book.

Buildings may have vertical supports like these, called **columns.** You may have thought wispy paper was too weak to hold a book. But paper can be strong if you use it right.

Columns can be thin. But when they are built right, they are strong enough to support a whole building.

Predict what would happen if you used fewer paper tubes. Then take them away, one at a time. You might need to rearrange the tubes as you go. At some point, your structure will collapse. How many tubes did you need to hold the book? Were your predictions right or wrong?

Now think back to the iScience Puzzle. Could you use paper columns to get the fruit across the water?

Congratulations! You just completed an experiment. This is how scientists test ideas.

As scientists work, they make careful records every step of the way.

In your experiment, you started with an idea about how a structure might be stronger than its parts. You tested the idea. Taking away columns allowed you to see what would happen to the book with different numbers of columns. You made a careful record of your actions as you worked. You did what a scientist does.

This student is testing ideas during an experiment.

Learning from Change

In a well-designed experiment, you will change only one thing. Everything else in the experiment must stay the same. That way, you can tell for sure whether the change you made caused another change. Say you took away a column and used a heavier book. The structure fell. You wouldn't know if fewer columns or a heavier book caused the structure to fall.

Thinking up and testing ideas is part of the **scientific method.** The process also includes asking questions, sharing ideas, and working with others. You should also be open to changing your mind if the results do not match your predictions.

Choosing Change

Maybe you want to build a boat for your grapefruit. Try this first. Gather two to four friends. You are a team. You will do this project together.

Materials

- deep sink (or basin) filled with 8 inches (20 centimeters) of water
- 80 marbles
- empty half-liter plastic water bottle with straight sides and a flat bottom
- tape
- waterproof marker

Be sure your bottle has straight sides, like the one shown here. You do not want a bottle that gets smaller near the middle.

Put a strip of tape down the side of the plastic bottle. The tape should reach to the very bottom. Use a waterproof marker to mark the tape every half centimeter, starting at the bottom. The bottle is your boat. Number the marks, starting with 1 at the bottom of the bottle. The marks will help you measure how well the boat floats.

Find a way to record information that will make sense to you when you read it again later.

Put 30 marbles into the bottle. Place the bottle into the water so the bottle opening is facing up. Be sure the bottle opening doesn't go underwater. When it's steady, jiggle it until it floats straight up and down. Record which mark is level with the water. This number is a measure of the depth of the bottom of the bottle.

In a notebook, describe and draw everything. Your notes might differ from someone else's. But they should remind you of how you set up the experiment.

You will add more marbles to the bottle. First, record a statement about what you believe will happen. Use your science background. In science, this guess is called a **hypothesis.** What do you think will happen when you add one more marble? What will happen when you add 50 more?

Now make a table or a chart. First, write down how many marbles are in the bottle. There are 30 to begin. Then, use the tape marks to record the depth of the bottom of the bottle.

One at a time, add marbles to the bottle. After every five marbles, write down the total number of marbles and the depth of the bottle.

Number of Marbles	Depth of Bottle
30	
35	
40	
45	
50	
55	
60	
65	
70	
75	
80	

Scientists often keep track of what happens during an experiment by making a table. A table can show how one thing in an experiment affects another thing. Your table should look like the one here. It shows how the number of marbles affects how much the bottle sinks in the water.

No one can look into the future. Scientists have to conduct careful experiments in order to answer questions.

Look at your results. How did the bottle move in the water? How much did it move? Explain why your hypothesis was or wasn't supported.

Think about the iScience Puzzle. If you make a boat, you will want it to float. How might adding weight affect your boat? After you build it, how will you test it?

Trial 1		Trial 2	
Number of Marbles	**Depth of Bottle**	**Number of Marbles**	**Depth of Bottle**
30		30	
35		35	
40		40	
45		45	
50		50	
55		55	
60		60	
65		65	
70		70	
75		75	
80		80	

Add to the table you made earlier so that it looks like this one.
Be sure you have the "Depth of Bottle" filled in for Trial 1.

In science, it is important to test ideas more than once. Maybe you made a mistake the first time around. Each time you run the experiment to collect a new set of data is called a **trial.** You can use trials to make sure that your data is good.

So try running another trial of this experiment. But first, talk to your teammates. How did you work together the first time? Did everyone participate? Was there a leader? On the next round, switch jobs. See if you can do the experiment more quickly. Did you find the same results in each trial?

What would happen to the birds in this nest if there were five baby birds instead of two? What other variables do you think would be affected?

Various Variables

Experiments are full of change. Things that change in an experiment are called **variables.** Some things you change on purpose, like the number of marbles in the bottle. These are **independent variables.**

Some things change as a result of what you do, like the depth of the bottle in the water. These are **dependent variables.** Knowing your variables can help you understand results.

Think about the paper columns. What was the independent variable? (What did you change?) What was the dependent variable? (What changed as a result of the change you made?)

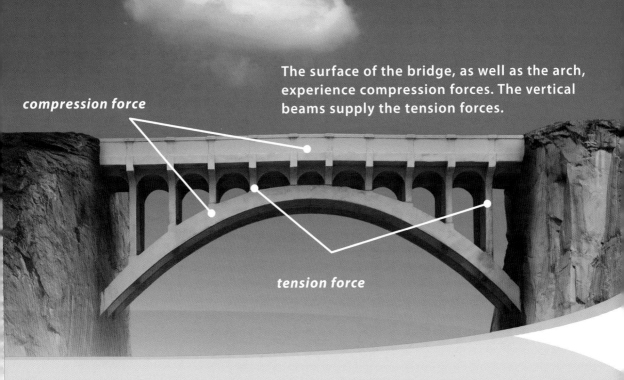

The surface of the bridge, as well as the arch, experience compression forces. The vertical beams supply the tension forces.

compression force

tension force

You are becoming an expert at experiments. You've formed hypotheses. You've worked with variables. And you've taken careful notes of the setup and results for each trial.

You've also worked on your building skills. You've seen what builders call **compression.** This is a squeezing or pushing force, like the book pushing down on the paper tubes. Building also involves a force that pulls. This is called **tension.**

Your iScience Puzzle project must stand up to compression, tension, and bending. Experiments will help you test each type of force.

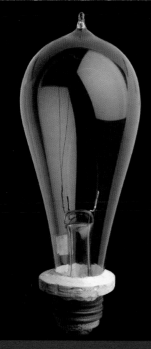

This early version of a light bulb was made by Thomas Edison.

CONNECTING TO HISTORY

Thomas Edison and the Light Bulb

If you are inside, there is probably a light bulb in the room. Today, electric lights are a big part of life. For that, we owe thanks to Thomas Edison.

Edison was an American inventor and scientist. He lived from 1847 to 1931. Starting in the 1870s, Edison and people who worked for him were part of a race to make the best light bulb. His first bulbs burned out after just a few hours. That was not useful for lighting a house.

Edison worked on electric lighting for more than a year. He had to do many experiments to find the best materials. And he looked at many variables. One variable he focused on was the filament. This is a thin strip of material that glows inside the bulb. He tried using the metal platinum as the filament. But platinum was expensive and did not work well. Then he tried carbon, which was cheap. But the bulb lasted less than 14 hours.

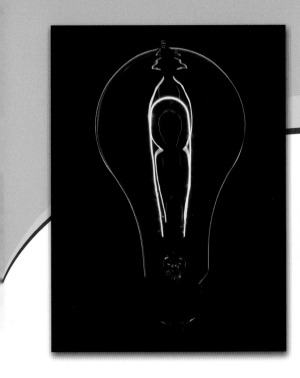

Here's another example of one of Edison's light bulb experiments.

So he did more experiments. This time, his variable was the source of carbon. He experimented with many materials that contain carbon. He tried paper, wood, bamboo, even coconut hair. Finally, he used strips of **carbonized cotton.** It worked best.

Edison worked on other parts of the bulb, too. Another variable was the kind of gas inside the bulb—or no gas at all, not even air. His best bulb had almost no air at all inside, which prevented the filament from burning.

Today, filaments in light bulbs are made of the metal tungsten. These bulbs are called incandescent. The bulbs may be filled with argon or halogen gases that do not burn easily.

Have you seen bulbs with no filaments? Examples are fluorescent and LED (light-emitting diode) lights. These light bulbs last longer and use less energy than incandescent bulbs.

How Do You Do an Experiment?

Experiments can be as fun as they are useful. You get to use your imagination. "Swing" on to the next activity to get a taste of the possibilities.

Could you build a swing with a long enough rope to get you all the way across the water? What would be tall enough to hang it from?

Build It

Think back to the river you want to get across to build your tree house. There might be trees along both banks. Maybe you could build a simple swing. Here is an experiment to test the idea. With your team, try it. Make sure to use the lessons you've learned about teamwork.

Materials

- string (about a foot long, or 30.5 centimeters)
- pile of books or magazines
- ruler
- 2 large paper clips
- 2 AA batteries
- tape
- stopwatch (or clock with a second hand)

Your pendulum setup should look like the one above. The two stacks of books need to be the same height. So try to use copies of the same books in each stack.

You may think of swings as fun things on a playground. But swings demonstrate several scientific principles. In science, a swing is a type of **pendulum.** It's a weight that hangs from a fixed point and swings back and forth.

For this activity, you will build a small pendulum. Tie one end of the string to a paper clip. Tape a battery to the paper clip. Then, tie the other end of the string to a ruler. Balance the ruler on two even stacks of books so that the string hangs down. The battery should hover about halfway between the ruler and the surface of the table. This is your pendulum. Imagine that it is swinging from one bank of a river to the other.

You have to time your pendulum's movement. It is important to make accurate measurements. Practice and teamwork can help.

stopwatch

Pull the battery toward you. Pay attention to how far you pull the pendulum back. This is your variable. Everything else should stay the same. When you let go, your battery should swing smoothly and freely.

Each time the battery goes back and forth, it finishes a **cycle.** As you watch it swing, watch the clock to see how long a cycle takes. Then make some predictions. What do you think would happen if you started by pulling the battery back even more? What if you didn't pull the battery back as far as you did the first time?

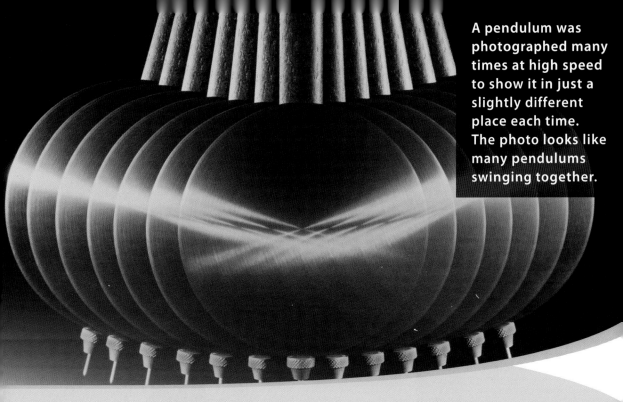

A pendulum was photographed many times at high speed to show it in just a slightly different place each time. The photo looks like many pendulums swinging together.

Organize your notes. Write down each step of what you have done. Draw your experiment. Record your predictions and create a table for your observations. You will want to keep track of the number of swings and the cycle time. What else do you want to write down? As you work, you might find better ways to keep track of your results.

Now, start the pendulum and the clock at the same time. You might want to work with a partner. That way, one person can watch the pendulum. The other can watch the clock.

With a stopwatch, you can measure exactly one cycle. You might want to measure five or ten cycles. Then, you can take the average. This will ensure that you are doing each trial the same way. Write down what you find.

See if your prediction was correct. What happens if you run more trials of the experiment? Do you get the same results each time? How did your team work together this time?

27

When you're on a swing, you become a pendulum!

There are many ways to change just one variable in this experiment. To begin, try pulling back the battery twice as far as you did in the first round. Then pull it back half as far as you did the first time. Record and compare both sets of results with the original.

Now try pulling back the battery three times as far as you did in the first round. Then, do it a third as far. Do you notice any patterns? Predict what will happen if you start with four times or one-fourth the distance. Do the experiment to see if you're right.

Don't take your pendulum down yet! More trials are coming up.

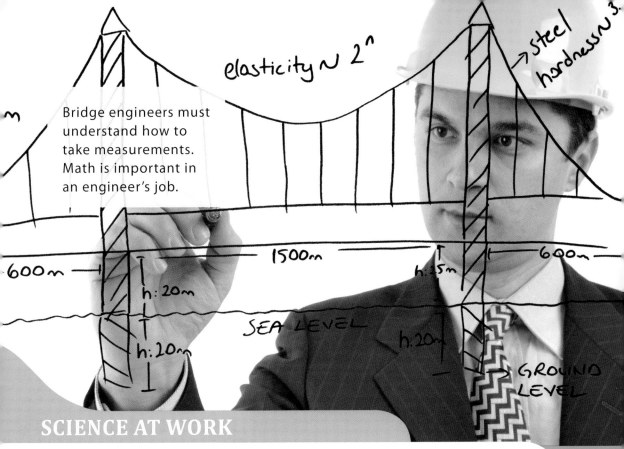

elasticity ~ $2^{\wedge}$

→ steel hardness ~ 3

Bridge engineers must understand how to take measurements. Math is important in an engineer's job.

600m

1500m

600m

h: 20m

h: 15m

h: 20m

SEA LEVEL

h: 20m

GROUND LEVEL

SCIENCE AT WORK

Engineer

Building blocks. Stacking cups. From an early age, kids love to design and create things. Engineers do it for a living. Engineers don't just build things and hope they work. They use math, science, and variables to make sure their projects are solid and safe.

There are many kinds of engineers. Civil engineers design bridges and dams. Environmental engineers help clean up hazardous waste sites, and develop rules that help prevent hazardous waste dumping in the first place. Biomedical engineers design devices such as artificial arms and legs. They help solve medical problems. Sometimes engineers create entirely new ways of doing things. Other times, they make existing objects work better.

Look around you. What do you see that might have been designed by engineers?

In Control

You've done a few experiments so far. In each activity, you changed one variable at a time. Then you watched what happened. Now think about the variables that stayed the same.

In the paper tube activity, for instance, you used the same book in every trial. In the boat activity, you kept the same amount of water in the sink. These are called controls, or **controlled variables.** You could have changed them, but you didn't.

Doing experiments is like conducting traffic. Cars will move safely as long as the officer controls which vehicles move at the same time.

Look at your pendulum experiment again. The only variable you changed is the distance your pendulum swings. That is the independent variable. Often, experiments have more than one controlled variable. What are the controls in your pendulum experiment? Keep reading to find out ways that the controls may become independent variables.

Some clocks are made with pendulums. They are good at keeping time. As you work through the experiment, think about why pendulums keep good time.

In the first round of trials, the weight of the pendulum didn't change. It was a controlled variable. Now make it an independent variable.

Tape the second paper clip to the second battery. Hang it with the first battery. You can do this by hanging one paper clip from the other clip. Or you can tie the string through both clips. Do you think the extra weight will change the pendulum's cycle time?

Make a note of the new steps in your notebook. Include your prediction. Then, measure the time of a cycle. Make sure to start the pendulum at the same distance that you used in the first round. Can you explain why this is a good idea?

Look at your results. Try to explain why your hypothesis was or was not supported.

A pendulum swings back and forth in a straight line that doesn't change. But as Earth spins, the floor under the pendulum spins, too. That makes it look like the pendulum's motion changes. You can see this false motion if the pendulum hangs above a surface with numbers on it. The pendulum appears to swing slowly from number to number over a day's time.

You've tested your pendulum in two ways. First you looked at the effects of swinging distance. Then you varied the weight. Now see what happens when you change the length of the pendulum.

First, take off the second battery so the weight is the same as it was in the first round. Then, predict how the time to complete a cycle will change if you make the string shorter. Also predict how it will change if you make the string longer.

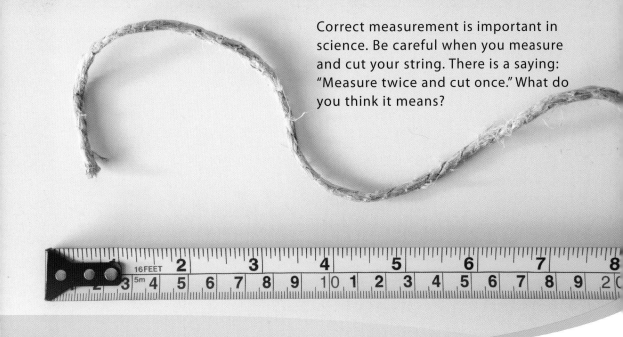

Correct measurement is important in science. Be careful when you measure and cut your string. There is a saying: "Measure twice and cut once." What do you think it means?

Try both. First measure the length of the string. In one trial, make it 50 percent longer. In another trial, make it 50 percent shorter than in the original experiment. If your string is 10 inches (25.4 centimeters) long after you've tied it at both ends, 50 percent longer would be 15 inches (38.1 centimeters) and 50 percent shorter would be 5 inches (12.7 centimeters). Remember to write everything down.

Now, talk to your team. Scientists usually present their findings to others. Discuss what you have learned. Try to understand why your hypothesis was or was not supported.

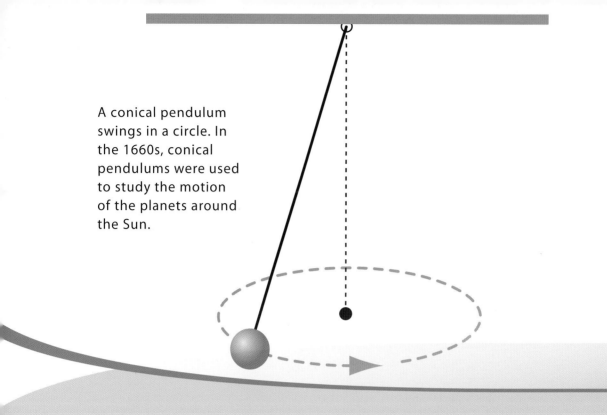

A conical pendulum swings in a circle. In the 1660s, conical pendulums were used to study the motion of the planets around the Sun.

Now, let your mind run free. When it comes to variables, you can do many things. Look at your pendulum. Write down all the independent variables you can think of, even if they seem silly. You might change the color or thickness of the string, for example. Or you could make the pendulum swing in a circle. That kind of pendulum is called a conical pendulum. When you are done, look through your list. Do you want to test any of your theories? Go for it. Scientists are always dreaming up and testing new ideas.

Finally, think about how you could use a pendulum to get across a river. Would you want your swing to be short or long? Would the weight of any materials you bring change your design? What are the pros and cons of this strategy?

see caption

Where would you put a pendulum on the riverbank to swing across the water?

Now consider your grapefruit in the sink. There are no "trees" next to the sink. To make a pendulum, you would need to build something to swing it from. Why would it be good and why would it be bad to build on the riverbank? Why would it be good and why would it be bad to build in the middle of the river?

Most big bridges are built with steel. This bridge was made with wood.

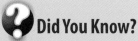

? Did You Know?

Bridges are supposed to hold the weight of whatever goes across them. This picture shows a bridge that was badly built. Why might a bridge fail?

35

Structure

There are lots of ways to cross a river. You've explored floating and swinging. Another strategy is to build a bridge. If you choose this option, you need to make sure the bridge is strong enough to hold both your tree house supplies and you. You could start with a **truss.** This is a type of framework that supports something.

Trusses are made from one or more triangles. They are stiff, so they are hard to bend. They are stronger than they look. Lots of houses have wooden trusses that hold up their roofs.

These trusses will hold up the roof of a house.

Many steel bridges are built with trusses. These bridges are strong enough to support trucks and buses. Look at the materials you have for the iScience Puzzle. What could you use to make a truss? How would you test your idea? Draw an experiment you could do to test the strength of a truss. If you have time, try it.

Remember, a grapefruit is the load you must move from one side of the water to the other.

You're a building machine! So far, you have made things that float, balance, and swing. You might have tried out trusses and bridges. If you have other ideas, check with an adult first to make sure they're safe. Then set up more experiments. Scientists always test their ideas before they start building.

Now look through your notes. Have any of your results helped you decide which way you want to get across the water? Do your ideas agree with those of your teammates?

How Do You Graph Results?

Still not sure what you want to build? Experiments can be useful, but sometimes it's hard to make sense of the results. **Graphs** can help. A graph is a diagram that shows data in a visual form. Instead of just listing numbers, a graph shows data as a picture.

Before you read more about graphs, guess what this graph is showing.

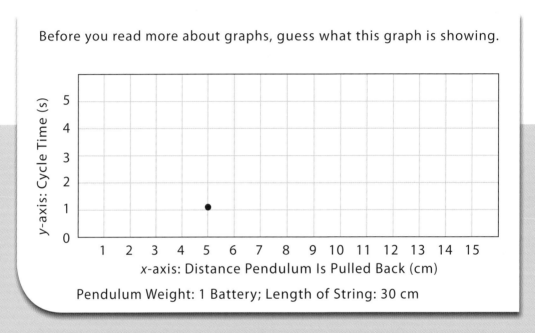

Pendulum Weight: 1 Battery; Length of String: 30 cm

On this graph, there is a **horizontal** axis, or *x*-axis. It shows how far the pendulum is pulled back, in centimeters. This is half of the full length of the swing made by the pendulum. It is the independent variable. The **vertical** axis is the *y*-axis. It shows time in seconds. This is the time it takes the pendulum to swing one cycle. It is the dependent variable.

When you make a graph, you need to label both axes with units. Notes explain the weight of the pendulum and the length of the string. Details are important. With labels and detailed notes, anyone who looks at the graph can understand it.

Making Sense of Numbers

Once you have drawn a graph, you can put the data into it. One way to start is to write each measurement as an ordered pair. The point in the graph shows the ordered pair of (5 cm, 1.1 s). That means a pendulum was pulled back 5 centimeters from the vertical position. It took 1.1 seconds to travel once back and forth.

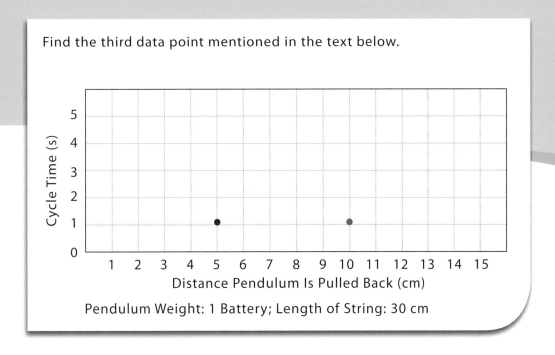

Find the third data point mentioned in the text below.

Pendulum Weight: 1 Battery; Length of String: 30 cm

Each ordered pair becomes a point on the graph. Go across to 5 cm on the *x*-axis and up to 1.1 s on the *y*-axis and place a dot. Say there is a second measurement on this graph, too. It is for (10 cm, 1.1 s). Does this result seem correct? Compare with your own data.

What if a third data point showed the result for 15 centimeters? How many seconds do you think it took for the pendulum to swing back and forth starting from this distance? Where would you plot the point on the graph?

Graphing your results can show you patterns that you might not have noticed if you only wrote down the numbers.

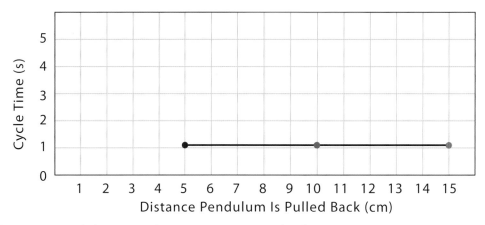

Results for One Trial of a Pendulum Experiment

Pendulum Weight: 1 Battery; Length of String: 30 cm

Here is a finished graph that someone made of the first trial of a pendulum experiment. All three points have been plotted on it. A line connects the points. How would you describe the line?

A graph can help you make predictions. First, look at the direction the line is going. Then extend the line. Now you can make good guesses about measurements you didn't take. How long will the pendulum take to swing one cycle if it starts from 12 centimeters?

This graph shows that the distance doesn't affect the time needed for one swing cycle. Look at the results of your other pendulum experiments. Were there any other variables that did not affect the cycle time?

Think about what you have learned in this experiment. Then think back to the pendulum clock shown on page 31. Why do pendulum clocks keep good time?

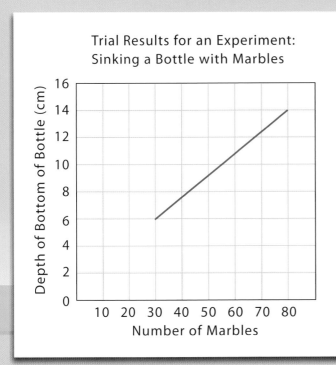

Trial Results for an Experiment:
Sinking a Bottle with Marbles

Depth of Bottom of Bottle (cm) vs. Number of Marbles

How deep was the bottle with 60 marbles in it?

The pendulum graph showed a straight, level line. Other graphs are more complex. The graph above shows the results from one trial of an experiment with marbles and a bottle floating in water.

This time, the line slopes upward. This means that the bottle sinks deeper as more marbles are added to it. Look at your results from the same experiment. Would your graph look similar? Try it and see.

Not all graphs produce straight lines. You can also end up with curves or even zigzags. Sometimes there is no pattern at all. That can tell you a lot, too. Often, it means that there is no measurable relationship between two variables.

Based on the graph, about how many seconds would it take a 150-cm-long pendulum to complete one full swing cycle?

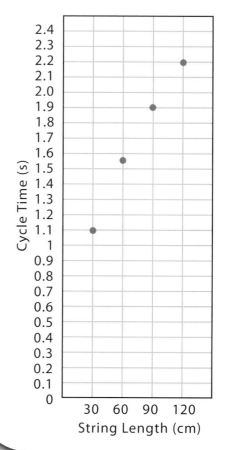

Trial Results for a
Pendulum Experiment

Now it's your turn to make sense of a graph. Take a look at the one above. It shows the results for one trial of a pendulum experiment. The length of the string is shown on the *x*-axis. The amount of time in a swing cycle is shown on the *y*-axis. You can see that doubling the length of the string did not double the time of a cycle. Neither did tripling the length.

About how much longer did the string have to be to double the cycle time? It may help to make a copy of the graph and draw a line through the data points. For what string length is the cycle time double the original value of 1.1 seconds?

You have considered a few ways to get your grapefruit across the sink. Each one has upsides and downsides.

You worked on a boat. This is a simple strategy. But too much weight could sink the boat. And it might be hard to paddle through waves or currents.

It might be fun to swing across like a pendulum. But this could be dangerous, too. The cord could snap, or you could fall. A bridge might be a more stable solution. You just need to make sure it won't collapse. What other ideas did you come up with? Which would be best for getting across a real river?

Any of these strategies could work. The key is to do enough experiments first. You may even want to build a model of your strategy. That way, you'll know if your idea is safe, within your budget, and sturdy. Once you've made your choice, build it and get the grapefruit across the water.

Using a bridge is a common way to get across a river. For the iScience Puzzle, you might have built a truss bridge with supports in the shapes of triangles. Or maybe you built a suspension bridge, where the main surface hangs from cables. If you had other materials, you could have built an arch bridge. The ancient Greeks and Romans built large arches from stone.

Using supplies you find at home or at school, design and build a bridge. Then add pennies or other objects, one by one, until the bridge breaks. Now try to make an even stronger bridge. What will your independent variables be? What are your dependent variables? What are your controls?

Look around you. What other questions do you have? How might you design experiments to answer them? The world is full of unsolved mysteries just waiting to be tested!

suspension bridge

carbonized cotton: cotton thread heated in the absence of air until it looks like charcoal.

columns: vertical pieces that help to hold up a building.

compression: a force that squeezes or pushes something together.

controlled variables: variables that are not allowed to change in an experiment.

cycle: a set of repeated patterns.

dependent variables: variables that change when another variable is changed.

experiments: the scientific procedures to test a hypothesis.

graphs: diagrams that show data in a visual form.

horizontal: with a straight side and having its length run from side to side.

hypothesis: a scientific idea that can be tested.

independent variables: variables that are changed to test a hypothesis.

pendulum: a weight that hangs from a fixed point and swings back and forth.

prediction: a description of what might happen in the future.

scientific method: a way to test a hypothesis using measurement, observation, and experimentation.

tension: a force that pulls.

trial: one run of an experiment to collect a set of data.

truss: a framework that supports something.

variables: things that change or are changed in an experiment.

vertical: with a straight side and having its length run up and down.

FURTHER READING

42eXplore, Bridge Building. http://42explore.com/bridge.htm

The BridgeSite, Fun and Learning. http://www.bridgesite.com/funand.htm

History for Kids! Pontoon Bridge.
http://www.historyforkids.org/learn/science/pontoon.htm

ADDITIONAL NOTES

Page 8: You wouldn't get wet crossing the river. You could cross back and forth without needing a boat. Building a bridge over a river takes a long time, costs a lot of money, and can be dangerous work.

Page 12: The paper tubes would get wet in the sink. Wet, soggy paper will not hold up much of anything.

Page 18: With more marbles, the bottle sank deeper into the water. Adding weight might make the boat sink too much.

Page 20: The independent variable was the number of paper tubes. The dependent variable was whether the tubes supported the book. Caption questions: Some of the baby birds would likely get more food than other baby birds. The amount of food would be the independent variable. The size and health of the baby birds would be the dependent variable.

Page 30: The controlled variables are the weight of the battery and the length of the string from which the pendulum hangs.

Page 34: You would want the string to be long. More weight means the string would have to be stronger. *Pros:* A swing would be much cheaper than a bridge, and would take less time to set up. *Cons:* If the river is wide, the string would have to be very long. There is probably nothing tall enough to hang it from. Falling off would be a danger. And how would you get yourself and your tree house supplies off the pendulum on the other side of the river?

Page 35: Building on the riverbank would be good because you are already there. But you are far away from the other side. And there may not be anything tall enough to hang the swing from. Building in the middle of the river would be good because you would be closer to the other side and so your pendulum could be shorter. But there is nothing to hang it from and you'd have to find a way to get yourself and your supplies to the middle of the river. Caption question: You'd want to hang your swing back away from the water. But that would put you in the bushes. Did You Know? question: A bridge may fail if its materials are not strong enough or if they are not put together properly.

Page 39: Yes. The distance is greater but the speed increased. It took 1.1 seconds. Plot the point at (15 cm, 1.1 s).

Page 40: The line is straight and horizontal. It will take 1.1 seconds. No, there were not any other variables that did not affect the cycle time. Pendulum clocks keep good time because no matter how far the pendulum is pulled back, the cycle time always stays the same.

Page 41: Caption question: With 60 marbles, the bottle was about 10.8 centimeters deep.

Page 42: The string had to be about 4 times longer to double the cycle time. It was 120 centimeters. Caption question: It would take about 2.5 seconds.

INDEX